819.1254 REI
PREZ : homage to Lester
Young /
Reid, Jamie, 1941-
891544 2010

VE JUN 2011
WK FEB 2016
SU MAR 2017
OS JUN 2017

PREZ

Homage to
Lester Young

NB APR 2011

WK FEB 2016

05 JUN 2017

PREZ

Homage to Lester Young

JAMIE REID

OOLICHAN BOOKS
FERNIE, BRITISH COLUMBIA, CANADA

Copyright © 1993 & 2010 by Jamie Reid ALL RIGHTS RESERVED. No part of this publication may be reproduced, stored in a retrieval system, or transmitted, in any form or by any means, without prior written permission of the publisher, except by a reviewer who may quote brief passages in a review to be printed in a newspaper or magazine or broadcast on radio or television; or, in the case of photocopying or other reprographic copying, a licence from ACCESS COPYRIGHT, 6 Adelaide Street East, Suite 900, Toronto, Ontario M5C 1H6.

New edition - 2010.

Library and Archives Canada Cataloguing in Publication

Reid, Jamie, 1941 -
    prez: homage to lester young/ Jamie Reid.

Poems
ISBN 978-0-88982-129-1

    I. Title.

PS8585.E43P7 1993   C811'.54   C1993-091479-1
PR9199.3.R449P7 1993

We gratefully acknowledge the financial support of the Canada Council for the Arts, the British Columbia Arts Council through the BC Ministry of Tourism, Culture, and the Arts, and the Government of Canada through the Canada Book Fund, for our publishing activities.

Published by
Oolichan Books
P.O. Box 2278, Fernie
British Columbia, Canada
V0B 1M0

Design by Carol and Jamie Reid and Oolichan Books with images by Carol Reid.

Printed in Canada on 100% post consumer recycled FSC-certified paper.

To My Friends

The Poets of Vancouver

Not forgetting Lester

Lester Young, nicknamed Prez by Billie Holiday because of his superb saxophone mastery, was the single jazz saxophonist who first held the key that opened the door to the room of modern jazz, a room later inhabited by the jazz genius, Charlie Parker and his musical friends and followers.

Lester was also a miraculous poet of the spoken idiom. The poetic inventions of his daily speech changed the spoken language of jazz and of North American popular music. He is said to be the first ever to use the word "cool" in its current hip meaning.

One year after the centenary of his birth, Lester remains too little known outside the world of jazz, even though the singing ephemeral pulse of his music can still be heard embedded in the playing of most of the greatest jazz saxophonists who have ever played since.

I am therefore delighted to be able to reprint this little book, my own homage to Prez, as a small means to help to keep the beauty of his musical legacy alive. The book has become the most popular and widely-read poem I've ever published. I believe this is mainly because of the human-made beauty that the special quiet genius of Prez brought into the world.

Jamie Reid, April, 2010

PREZ

"Just all music, all day and all night music.
Just any kind of music you play for me,
I melt with all of it."

LESTER YOUNG

"He was the most beautiful man, the trunk of the
swing tree, I would like to say. No Prez - no Bird, no
Dexter, no Coltrane, no Miles either.
Prez was truly the master of time and space,
nuances and understatements."

JOHNNY GRIFFIN

I

Rhapsody: Lester's Sound

Here are notes like the motes of the last dappled sunlight,
  melting like gold on the clusters of leaves.

Here too is the singing light of the dawn on the same leaves,
  reawakened in the eyes of the man who has not slept
  throughout the night.

Here are the first stars of the evening like emeralds embroidered
  on velvet, and here are the last stars of the morning,
  like ice melting on silk.

Here is the light in the smoke of the nightclub, where the
  feelings of lovers and lonely ones float to the ceiling
  in spirals.

Here is their love of the music, which they cling to because
  they despair of anything else to rescue the human heart.

Here is the sound of the heart purely in love, loving nothing
  in particular, but all of the particulars of the world
  in which that heart is alive and beating.

Here is the sound of the heart and breathing, alive to the nuance
  of just this precise unalterable moment and no other.

Here is the joy of pure desire which desires nothing
  but to be lost amongst all of the things which are.

Here is the permanent moment of rain remembered.

Here is the flurry of notes like snow, strangely warm, into which
    the voice of a woman suddenly enters to comfort you,
    but which is just as suddenly smothered again.

Here is the ache of the air from which her voice has been
    so cruelly withdrawn.

Here is the milky luminescence of fog spread and reflected,
    droplet by droplet of wet, until nothing is seen but
    that silvery shining, the same as it was at the beginning
    of things.

Beyond this, there is a darkness barely seen, beyond which again
    is another and more perfect darkness unseen.

Here is the pit-a-pat-pat of counting, in which the spaces
    between the numbers are never the same length
    and are never the same shape either.

Here is the moment when time stops and goes back on itself,
    when all the gestures and reachings of past life
    are repeated as though in a film reversed.

Here is the single damaging phrase flashing like a tongue
    of terrible flame into the darkened room
    where a door has been opened by surprise.

Here is the flickering static of atoms and electrons jostling,
    sounds which began their journey to earth
    ten million years ago and more.

Here is the annihilating honk of the great black holes in space,
  ravening for loose matter and light, so dense with being
  they annihilate all being, all becoming and all knowing.

Here is the drone and cry of the creatures beneath the sea,
  the clatter of billions of claws drowned in sea water.

Here is the love between particular men and women,
  transcending sex and generation, but locked in that same
  shuddering medium out of which the new is constantly coming,
  smelling like roses.

Here are the eyes of the trees glancing at you without smiling
  and without pain.

Here are dresses and suits lined up in racks on a city street,
  the shoes piled in bins, which will never be worn,
  while barefoot men and women are walking
  the sides of the river, half-naked and hungry.

Here is the sound of coins in the pocket. Taken into your hand,
  they speak with an echo of Hammurabi and Caesar, and of
  the old man recently found dead in the street.

Here, strangely, there are no flowers, except for the odor
  of those roses, and a single very white gardenia,
  perched in a woman's hair.

Here is the sound of water wherever it appears. In its lapping,
you hear the sound of languages unwritten and forgotten.

But here too is the voice of a language not yet spoken
by a race of men and women not yet born.

"He used to have a saying: 'All the physicians come to hear the musicians!' We should bring some beauty into the world. When you play for the people you can all yourself great all you want. You are not great until the people say you are. And when the people say you're great, you don't argue about that. You say: 'Thank you!' And that's what I was taught."

WILLIE JONES

II

Lester died on purpose. The president
   could not command the real world
      to behave
according to his imagination
  of what it ought to be
      and what he knew it could be, because
of what he knew
of what he was himself,
and what he knew
of what he wished
he might at last become.

"Hear this," he'd say—
and then he'd play it
note for note so they all could hear.
But they didn't hear it
as he played it—
in the same way
that what he thought he heard
was different
from the way he played it.

**THIS IS ONLY THE ECHO THIS IS ONLY THE
ECHO THIS IS ONLY THE ECHO THE ECHO
THE ECHO OF WHAT I HEAR I HEAR I HEAR
AND WHAT YOU HEAR IS ONLY THE ECHO
THE ECHO THE ECHO OF WHAT I PLAY I
PLAY I PLAY.**

"Well," he said, *"these persons want to make money out of me. As soon as I die there'll be some memorial albums out on me."*

REVEREND JOHN GENSEL

"The greed of the few people that wanted to play God and control everything, they deprived the world of such great beauty, and that's one of the reasons why he died."

WILLIE JONES

III

Poor Lester put on his best grey suit and called for the barber to come to his house and cut his hair because he had decided to die and expected his friends to come and pay their respects at the last.

Lester acted this way not out of respect for death, but out of fear for what the living would think of him should he go to his grave with his hair uncut and his suit unpressed. Even in death, he was a professional.

Lester always had money. Well, not always, but later in life he always had money. He made more money than any man alive in his profession while he was alive and he continues to make money for others even today while he rots in the grave.

Lester was never a rich man because he gave all his money away.

He kept his sidemen alive so that when the time was ripe, they could play with him again. He'd sidle up to them like a thief from the shadows where they stood at the bar hungering for a drink or a gesture and say to them, "Have yourself a good time man," slipping them half a yard and slipping away before they could protest or refuse or even say thanks.

"His playing was a tremendous adventure all the time. There was always a surprise, and he was a great virtuoso, one of the great virtuosi of jazz. There are not that many that are great musically as well. He also represented a new kind of person in the American community, which later evolved as something we call 'cool' or 'hip.' He was a poet, too, a great poet."

JOHN LEWIS

"He was a living, walking poet. He was so quiet that when he talked each sentence came out like a little explosion."

JOHN LEWIS

Lester invented his own language because he was bored with the words and meanings of the words of the language he had already heard and the world he had already seen.

He used words like candles to illuminate the hidden corners where nobody else was ever looking. Lester then slowly taught this language to everybody else who could hear him, and millions who couldn't. But it was not the words he wanted to teach. It was the habit of looking into corners.

Lester was the original inventor of the world cool, and he invented the word while jazz was still hot.

Lester was the most relaxed man on earth. When somebody spoke in the ordinary language of curses and slurs, Lester said, "I feel a draft," and then he would leave the room because the draft was uncool.

Lester invented the word threads to describe a suit of clothes. In the same way, Democritus invented the word atoms to describe the matter which surrounds us and of which we are made.

"Don't call the chords to me, just play the chords and I'll play."

LESTER YOUNG

Lester called his horn a motherfucker,

because Lester would not be
what somebody else already was
Lester would not be
Lester would not
Lester would be
Lester would be
Lester.

IV

Lester's language is the language
of people who do not sleep at night.
Being guilty of nothing, they still
cannot sleep, because,
like children,
they are always desiring
what they cannot have.

Ray Charles was not born blind.
Staring at the sun at the age of three,
he says he burned his eyeballs, connected
to his brain.
"I loved that motherfucker," he said,
"My mother said I'd go blind,
and I did."

What did he want?
Did he want the blinding summer light of Georgia,
or the permanent night of New York?

The night is supposed to be quieter than the day.
But not in New York, where some people
never sleep.

"We the whores, Socks."

LESTER YOUNG, TO BOBBY SCOTT

*"I set my own tempos, and I take my time.
I wish jazz were played more often for dancing.
I have a lot of fun playing for dances because I like to
dance, too. The rhythm of the dancers comes back to
you when you're playing."*

LESTER YOUNG

The waking heads of men in daytime,
Heraclitus said, are turned toward
the self-same light, while in the night
their sleeping heads are turned
towards as many darknesses
as there are heads.

Lester worked the nightshift and kept his eyes half-open
so people would believe that he was half-asleep.
One half dreaming, one half wide awake,
he saw everything,
including all those tunnels into the darkness.

He had to work the nightshift,
because the ones from whom he took his orders—
King Oliver, Count Basie, Billie Holiday—
also worked at night.

Then there were the listeners,
in America, supposed to be the real boss.
Who did not need Lester to listen to.
Who were only in love with the beat
and what it did to their feet.
Dancing until the dust rose in clouds from the floor,
they put sweet rhythms into Lester's horn.

Later, when everybody fell exhausted into bed,
Lester listened to the sound of the lightbulbs buzzing
in the hotels where they allowed him to stay:
WHAW-WHAH-WHAW-WHAW—the buzzing of the blues,
     the sound
of dead jazzmen, still paying their dues.

These apparent necessities and certainties
do not yet explain
the after-hours sessions in the cities
where unpaid jazzmen tested out each others powers.
Some sank, some floated,
and some flew right away.

Nor do they explain the sounds
from country woodsheds,
where poor jazzmen, unemployed,
bent their heads and blew their brains out
and emerged alive.

V

Lester and Billie Holiday
loved each other
like no other two human beings.
They loved each other
while each was in love with others.
They were like sister and brother.

People said they were like
Siamese twins
joined at the head.

Lester would outline a figure or a line
or rather half a figure, half a line
and then Billie would sing the other half
word for word and note for note,
never having heard before what Lester played.

Four lines later, all the others,
Buck, Mal, Jo, Teddy, or whoever else was there
would come in for the chorus,
which by this time
was completely obvious.

On ten different nights,
it would be obvious
ten different ways.

"The indefinable charm that is all Lester Young's own comes chiefly from his astonishing muscular relaxation. Good jazzmen have always had to be supple, but Lester has gone beyond being merely supple to achieve a kind of relaxation that has become something of a cult among his disciples . . ."

ANDRÉ HODEIR

VI

Lester is the opposite
of Dexter.

Dexter
is the right hand man, the man
whose every move is right, the move
that is required
at any time,
in any given situation.

Lester
is the left-hand man,
who speaks with a lisp or a stutter
and understands nothing
of what is ever said to him.

Lester dances to a different drummer
and never pays the piper, because
he is the piper.

Lester, in all his life,
was never late for a date.
This comes as no surprise,
because Lester was known all his life
as one of the slowest men alive.

Even when he was late,
Lester was always
right on time.

*"It's got to be sweetness, man, you dig?
Sweetness can be funky, filthy, or anything, but which
part do you want?"*

LESTER YOUNG

VII

Lester drank
   the fermented fruit
      of the juniper tree, letting
the fumes of this potion,
   or poison, seep
      into the cells of his brain,
where it mixed with his pain
   to create that sweet, foggy ease.

What came up was then not pain,
   but balm, incense, clouds
      of pleasure, air, fragrance, the breath
         of infants and their easiest laughter.

There was also the laughter
   of knowing adults, knowing
      better than to weep,
because weeping creates only weeping,
   while laughter
      creates life.

In the silence of that night,
Lester was listening, listening
to the slow, easeful gestures of women
deeply in love, listening
to the music of their conversation
when they were alone together
without men. Listening, listening…

That helpless,
   knowing laughter.

VIII

Lester is patient and takes the time to frame each note
and phrase and link it with the note and phrase which
went before and the ones which will come after.

The notes, like molecules of water, always the same,
move within a stream, or rest as though in a lake, or
shoot up in a fountain, imitating flame.

Lester is patient with the music and takes his time,
laying on his notes as a painter lays on colour, layer
by layer until the picture is logically complete and
glowing--perfect, as it were, or as it will be, then, when
the world of people will at last look differently, all its
ordinary ugliness within the mirror of the music all
transformed.

Being impatient with the real world, Lester takes his
time to make the music perfectly and so transform that
real world.

"As far as I'm concerned, I think Coleman Hawkins was the President, first, right? When I first heard him, I thought that was some great jazz I was listening to. As far as myself, I think I am the second one. No braggadocio, you know. I don't talk like that. There's only one way to go. If a guy plays tenor, he's got to sound like Hawk or like Lester."

LESTER YOUNG

IX

Lester Speaks

You think I do this
    because I like it—
stay up all night, drink
    until my head aches and my hand shakes,
speak politely to strangers
    who are blind
        to what is right in front of their eyes,
whose very word
    is ignorance and insult;
        spend every blessed night
    waiting to hear
        and then to reproduce
that sound,
    the sound which approaches the sound
        of a real human being,
instead of this incessant
    barking and clucking.

You mean
    I have to feel like this,
        so somebody else
            can feel wonderful?

Some of them even have the nerve
    to worship me.

I know,
    I ain't no dog, but
        I ain't no angel either.

I've got all that I can do
    just to pretend
        that I am
            a real living man.

Dogs bark. Chickens
    cluck. Men
    speak.

All I do
    is feed words into the saxophone:
warm words, hard words, cold words, hot words, round words, fat
words, colored words, words of love, funeral words, sharp words,
pointed words, words like burps and farts.

I shape my lips just right, and from my lungs, I push
this thread of air right through this reed, and then,
I move my fingers, bending air inside this tube, my horn,
and it all comes out here,
and goes in there.

I don't expect to be understood, because
I don't understand it myself. Understanding
is not the point. Poetry
is the language of the country
beyond the understanding.

Do not understand that I understand
that the world is not real. If
the world is not real, why
do I want it different from what it is? why
do I dream of another and a better place
that is not Hawaii or heaven,
but is this same New York in which I live
and feel like this?

If I had made this world up,
it wouldn't be like this, you
would not be living the way you do,
and me neither. I play
because there is nothing else to do,
and nothing else to be.

I drink to remember what I am and to forget
what I am not. I forget
that I am not Beethoven or Mozart or Bach,
or even Debussy, who are real heroes of civilization.

I am only Lester, a poor left-handed black man
whom even the army wanted to forget.
They gave me a rifle, and took away my saxophone.
They said I was anti-social, and when I raised my voice,
they put me in a cell.

The rifle
has a single trigger. Press this
and a man is dead. How powerful, it can make
wives and children weep.

The saxophone
carries 18 to 21 brass keys,
and as many keys of harmony
as two and a half octaves can contain.

Press these keys, people dance
and dream of children
and the means to keep them alive.

A Note of Thanks

"Apart from Lester, only three men, Armstrong, Parker and Coltrane, have had such a devastating effect on the sound of jazz as it is played by musicians at every level of competence. As Lester's sound, mediated particularly through the recordings of Stan Getz, spread in ever widening circles, it entered deep into the fabric not only of jazz but of popular music in general. Whenever a tenor saxophone emerged briefly from the ensemble of a dance band or light orchestra it spoke with the same accent."

DAVE GELLY, *Lester Young*

When I was writing this poem in 1987, the only full-length biography I could find was Lewis Porter's *Lester Young* (Twayne Publishers, 1986). While preparing for the publication of this chapbook, I first encountered Mr. Porter's excellent collection of essays and articles about Lester, entitled *A Lester Young Reader*, published by the Smithsonian Institute Press, Washington, D.C.

At that time, too, I first encountered Dave Gelly's wonderful short biography, *Lester Young*, (quoted above). It was first published in the U.K. in 1984 by Spellmount, Ltd., and by Hippocrene books of New York.

Frank Buchmann-Möller's *You Just Fight for Your Life, The Story of Lester Young* (Praeger, New York, 1990), also provided me with fresh insights.

In the interim between the first and second editions of this book, Douglas Henry Daniels published *Lester Leaps In: The Life and Times of Lester "Pres" Young* (Beacon, 2002), the most exhaustive biography that I have seen.

I wish I could have seen all of these books sooner, because they would have helped make my poem better.

The quotations throughout these pages were taken from one or another of these valuable works. I am very grateful to the authors and publishers of these fine books for making available important knowledge about the great American musical artist, Lester Young, whose greatness is too little recognized.

My grateful thanks to Bertrand Tavernier and everyone associated with *Round Midnight*, a beautiful film about the art and life of jazz, which was one of the earliest and most powerful inspirations for this poem.

JAMIE REID, April, 1993

Photo by Carol Reid

Homage to Lester Young was first published by Oolichan Books in 1993. Its author, Jamie Reid, was one of the five original editors of TISH, the Vancouver poetry newsletter that changed the face of Canadian poetry in the early 1960s. He is the author of four volumes of poetry, beginning with *The Man Whose Path Was on Fire*, in 1969. *Prez* was written in 1987 after Reid was absent for nearly two decades from publishing poetry while engaged in revolutionary political activism. It was followed by *Mad Boys* in 1997, and then by *I. Another. The Space Between* in 2004.

Diana Krall, The Language of Love, Reid's commercial biography about the celebrated Canadian jazz artist, appeared in 2002. He is also the author of several chapbooks, most recently *homages* from Pooka Press, a suite of poems based on his readings of modern French poetry. During the early 1990s, he produced and edited DaDaBaBy, a Dadaist-oriented magazine of poetry and commentary. He is widely published in anthologies, little magazines and electronic media. Currently he edits two poetry blogs: Schroedinger's Cat (www.canitplease.blogspot.com) and Remembering Gerry Gilbert (www.gerrygilbert.blogspot.com).

OKANAGAN REGIONAL LIBRARY
3 3132 03153 4557